there is room for all of you here

michaela angemeer

michaelapoetry.com | @michaelapoetry

Artwork by Michaela Angemeer

ISBN: 978-1-7752727-5-5

for jess

i never trusted forever
but now i trust you

i don't wanna write about
heartbreak anymore

contents

stumbling

[ˈstəmb(ə)liNG]
verb

> 1. to trip or lose one's balance for a moment;
> almost fall
> 2. pass into a specified state, situation, or position

sweet boy,
don't make me feel seen
you know the only thing
i like more than hating men
is male validation
every man in my life
has made it too easy for you
they'd rather hold hands
with the patriarchy
than try to empathize with me
but you got me right away
so please could you take me seriously
you have the upper hand
could i borrow the advantage
just this once

the bottom of this beer looks like
i love you
and i'll forget tomorrow
i thought i was done with this cycle
i thought i was ready for availability
turns out my heart is still cracked
turns out there's not enough blood
to keep me alive for much longer
turns out i'm still the unavailable one

i might always be the unavailable one

i keep confusing feeling understood
with someone understanding
how to manipulate me

am i cooler than your wife
do you think about it sometimes

my twenty-three to your thirty-four
underdeveloped frontal lobe
naan bread
if only i got it then

drunk trivia night
without your wife
cab driver asked
if you were my boyfriend

you might have been the one
who started this pattern
fanned my unrequited love
because you liked the attention

but i hope it makes you feel
less special to know
you made me feel the same
as everyone unavailable who came after

all of my crushes are in relationships
i only want stability
when it's holding up someone else

was it codependency
or was i in love
with all my former female friends
romance blindfolded by
compulsory heterosexuality
always ignored what was right in front of me
only seeking unavailable men
thinking i had to try to get them to love me
when i could've just been gay instead

i'm three months from thirty
and i still can't cry without a laugh
making my sadness palatable
has become second nature
minimizing it
like it's not there all the time
hiding with a smile
even when i'm the only one there to see it

before my birthday
i miss everyone i've ever known
even though i don't know them anymore
my life flashes before my eyes
usually the bad parts
i'm never sure if i'm dying
or just getting older
maybe it's all the same

i would be more upset that
you forgot about me
if i didn't forget about me too

my short term memory's fried
but i can still tell you everyone
who wronged me as a child

if i eat off of my childhood plates
one more time
i swear i'll time travel
become the smallest i've ever been
afraid to take up space again

my brother's house
feels like visiting my tomb
she was only seventeen
the plates we used to eat
leftover spaghetti
the couch still has my stain
fifteen-year-old nail polish
the glasses i filled
tap water at midnight
the same lampshade
designed in 1978
when i'm there i can hear her lifeless body
screaming
or maybe she's just letting out air
either way my brother doesn't hear her
either way he doesn't care

if i'm the only one trying
how do we heal the bonds between us

i feel overwhelming grief for my father
life turned out in a way he never planned
slammed on its breaks
flipped his car
more than once
you can't outsmart a cycle
if you're too afraid to watch it spin
and i've never been steel enough
to jam the spokes for him
a bloodline made of twigs
splintered fingers from birth
i'm grieving my father
but he's still alive
and i don't know if i'll have
any feelings left when he dies

if being misunderstood is an extreme sport
i am free climbing at three thousand feet
bloody fingertips
strained neck
there's no way you can hear me scream
but if you could
you'd swear i was whispering

do we accept the love
we think we deserve
or do we accept the love
we were taught we deserved

my grandparents have been dying for years
and my voice is too high-pitched
for them to hear me say *rest in peace*
while they grow older
i stay the same age
i can't be another thing that's changed
all they know about me is that i'm alive
they pretend i still talk to mom
and see her when i cry

i'd much rather get the news
that someone has died
than someone is dying
i don't have the words for this part
and the only thing worse
than saying goodbye
is standing in the doorway for an hour

sorry i couldn't make it to your funeral
i was in mexico
and i don't wear black anymore
i think mom forgave you
or swallowed it down
but i couldn't
and i won't
and i don't believe in
heaven or hell
but if you're with nana
i hope you're treating her better
i hope you're treating her well

dear yayo

i know you don't know
what no contact means
your biweekly letters
are in my spam folder
and your dog wished me
happy birthday

i know you don't see
me as anything but
an extension of yourself
my individuality makes you nauseous
but still you'd rather belittle
than look in the mirror

i know you don't have
the courage to dig deeper
to understand why
after twenty-seven years
i couldn't take it anymore
i could no longer try

whipping boy

i miss my mom the most
when i'm sick
she never saw me whole
but she knew
how to love something
that needed fixing

i don't wanna live up to my parents' expectations
so they know how it feels
it's too bad they taught me
how to please everyone but myself
sit, down, stay
i was always obedient
until i strayed
i wonder if their new dog
is a good boy
i wonder if he's doing a good job
of replacing me

what is my
peace worth?

both patriarchs in my family are dead
but i'm afraid i've inherited their narcissism

no i don't know how it feels
to grow up feeling safe
i didn't learn how to feel my feelings
until twenty-eight

now i know
i was scared all the time
good morning
always laced with landmines

a glass of red wine
with supper
a snide remark
i didn't understand

i thought by thirty
i would be able to let go
forgive and forget
or at least move on

but the truth is you can still see
shrapnel in my smile
can still hear
eggshells when i walk

the only difference is now
i get to be angry
and i think part of me
always will be

check engine light on permanently
inside my body
i thought two years of therapy
would equal more than lifting up the hood
and still not knowing what i'm looking for
i thought i wouldn't be able to
operate with a cracked heart
but i drove thirty thousand miles
is it in my gut?
(i know it's in my gut)
but what about the tightness in my right calf?
the knot in my left shoulder blade?
the way my jaw clicks?
can somebody make it a little more obvious
i can't sleep with this light on

i have complicated feelings about everything

though the men in my family
will never really understand
at least they pick up when i call
witness my growth
listen when i speak
none of us are perfect
but i'm glad they're here
we won't always get it right
but at least we're still trying

why do i have to make
my anger agreeable
like i'm not allowed to be mad
unless i immediately tie it up in a bow

i keep sliding between
earnest and nihilist
i need to mop up the floor
everything is either meaningful
or meaningless
once again i can't stand
cause i've never known balance
forever stumbling

when you spend your whole life
doing things you don't want to do
it's hard to stop

falling

['fôliNG]
verb

1. move downward, typically rapidly and freely
without control
2. throw oneself down, often in order to worship or
implore someone

i like when you smell good
and your hair is clean
a soft voice
a long laugh that comes with tears
i like the look you get
before you tell a joke
the way you tap your foot
when you're nervous
i like how you smile
when you talk about your friends
the way you don't go anywhere
without a pen
i like how you're grumpy
when you're hungry
that you're a generous tipper
who's good with money
but i can't see that
no i can't see any of that
in a photo you took on vacation
two years ago

everyone keeps reinforcing my belief that
people are unreliable
can't someone be consistent for once
can't one person stick to their word
not make me second guess
or double check
i'm not asking for much
just don't say you'll be there
if you have no plan to

my trust issues are a self-fulfilling

PROPHECY

just when i thought i got used to everyone leaving
more people are planning their departures
and i can't do another goodbye
instead i'm waiting at arrivals
for the next friend who feels like family
the next person i'll love
the person i'll become now that you're gone

date yourself. affirm yourself the way you would want a partner to. hug yourself when you cry. listen to yourself. ask the questions you're afraid to answer. reassure yourself. trust yourself. plan solo trips and go on them. celebrate friendships and chosen family more than you ever have. buy yourself a birthday present for the first time. flowers for no reason. romanticize everything you do by yourself. teach yourself how you want to be loved, and how deserving you are of it.

i refuse to believe that
i don't get to choose
how i'm loved

is it self-sabotage
if it's in my dna
women hiding for generations
all i hear is
hundred-year-old echoes of
it's not safe to be yourself

we can be brave now
i scream back

we can trust ourselves
i scream back

we can love who we love
i won't stop screaming

i hope you know that being open to love again after giving up on it is one of the greatest acts of bravery. even though you're terrified, you are so courageous. i know vulnerability feels like prying your chest open with scarred palms, but what if it's worth it? what if you find someone just as soft as you. what if you find someone who knows you don't deserve to be discarded. what if being seen becomes effortless. what if feeling doesn't have to hurt. what if they make everything you've been through worth it. what if they teach you how to love again.

is finding someone that scary
is falling that terrifying
if all you have to gain is love
and even if you lose it
you'll be left
just as whole as you were
with a new appreciation
for how someone else can love you
like you love you

there is

room

for all

of me

here

when it was cloudy for six days straight
you were the sun

i wanna buy you a side table
even though you've never been in my bed
where's the line between hopeful
and unhinged
i don't wanna make the same mistakes again

i don't wanna move too fast
but i do have an extra toothbrush

i don't wanna move too fast
but should we get matching tattoos

i don't wanna move too fast
but do you want to go to chicago

i don't wanna move too fast
but do you want to uhaul

i don't wanna move too fast
but do you want to love me

i wonder if i'm the first person
you called sunshine
or kissed three times
is this new to you too
or is this what olivia was referring to
when she wrote *deja vu*

when i wrote
i think i could love you
on your back with my fingertip
did you feel it
could you love me too

hurting you would
hurt me more

i've been by myself for so long
that when i feel off balance
it's instinctual to push you away
but i don't want you to leave
i need you to stay

i'm sorry did i confuse you
with my inconsistency
if we're still together in three years
we should get married
but i'm not sure i ever want to live with somebody
i wanna see you every minute of every day
but i also wanna be alone
to pluck the chin hairs on my face
do you wanna adopt my dog
or never see me again
sometimes i forget we're more than just friends
i want to blame my gemini placement
or my mom and dad
but honestly i don't know why
my mind changes every time the wind blows
and my mood changes as often as the tide

i'm trying to think my way out
of things i need to feel instead
my brain tells me
to catch myself
cause it doesn't know the difference
between self-protection and destruction

i'm tripping over the future
right now is cloudy
and there's no chance of sun
i wish i could just be happy
with what's right in front of me
but i keep looking ahead
hold my face in your hands
make me look right at you
tell me there's beauty
in the journey
tell me i don't have to worry
about the destination

maybe we're not doomed
we just need to eat a vegetable
sit with the sun on our face
call a friend
take a walk
or a deep breath
hold someone's hand
drink a glass of water
smell a freshly cut flower
take a shower
maybe there's nothing to be afraid of anymore

what if

it just

all

works

out

where is the line between
advocating for myself
and trying to control someone else

why did my parents
not provide love consistently
it's already hard for me
to feel like myself
when you're not with me

are you staying over tomorrow
i don't wanna wash my sheets
until i know when
they'll smell like you again

maybe the other shoe won't drop
maybe you're wearing it
maybe i trust you because
i finally know what's good for me to hold on to
maybe the steps we walk together are worth it
maybe it doesn't matter where we end up
maybe all that matters is right now

i wanna be softer than
i've ever been for you

when you whispered
can i?
my heart skipped a beat
no one else ever asked
no one else ever cared if i said yes

i bought you a side table
if you leave
i'll throw it out immediately
i'd rather love you like i mean it
than be too scared to try

it's been less than a month
and i've already dedicated
this book to you
i don't want to be irrational
but i don't think either of us
has felt like this before
if my heart says you're the one
and my head knows it's true
why hold back
when i could just fall for you

this time i told my friends
this time i saved your number
this time i thought about the future
this time i cried tears of joy
this time i felt everything

i didn't know you existed
six weeks ago
but now you're making me pancakes
kissing my forehead
buying me flowers
calling me honey
singing my favourite songs
if you keep this up
i might start to think
that being with you
is better than being solo

i wanna be
so gentle with you

one day you'll wake up and realize that all the work you did was worth it. that excavating every little part of you, and telling every last bit not to hide. telling every little piece of yourself you've ever been ashamed of that it deserves love too. one day you'll meet someone who mirrors it all back to you. and you'll be able to love in a way you never have before. because instead of looking for the cracks, instead of seeing their humanness as a flaw like you saw yours for so many years, all that love and understanding you cultivated for yourself will radiate onto them. and you'll have your first love where loving them doesn't mean loving yourself less. you'll have your first love where loving them means loving yourself even more.

look at how you've grown
even without the sun

i can't believe i found you
i can't believe it happened
and i'm petrified
cause i've never been this happy

landing

['landiNG]
verb

1. an instance of coming or bringing something to land
2. going or bringing to a surface after a voyage or flight

everything was hard
until we found each other

i wanna give you a soft life

you're making me believe
in the impossible
like people can be reliable
and consistent
and stick to their word
i've stopped second-guessing
and double-checking
i don't have to ask anymore
cause when you say you'll be there
it's true

you rewrote all my old poems
erased the hurt
made me feel like love was always this easy
and now everything i've ever written
is about you

how

are

you

real

play with my hair
the wrong candle
leftover pizza
coffee to go
kiss me in threes
soft hands
cookie delivery
tiger's eye
matching playlists
two cars in the driveway
miss you already

girlfriends

dear passersby,
please forgive this dumb
look on my face
i'm just in love and
i can't stop thinking about them

when you kiss me
i feel it in every part of my body

i wrote a letter to my future love
put it under a candle
made a wish
two years later i opened it up
and couldn't help but cry
because as i was becoming
everything i wished for
so were you

to the love of my life:

thank you for bringing joy into every day. your laugh and boundless energy make my life so much better. i love learning and growing with you. and that every day is its own little adventure. i am so grateful for your deep caring and understanding. i just wanna get to know you until the end of the earth. thank you for never failing to surprise me in the most beautiful ways that make me feel more loved than i've ever felt. your presence is a gift. your mind is a wonder that unravels in the most profound ways. i just want to live inside your brain. you bring depth to the moments that need quiet and light to the moments that deserve celebration. i love that you lead with love and are so aware of the impact you have on other people. i am so honoured to call you my partner and best friend. the idea of our life together is the most exciting thing i've ever imagined.

TO THE MOON
AND BACK

you're my favourite smell
and i like holding your hand
we have the same interests
and you listen to all my plans
you're soft with yourself
and understanding too
you're aware of your needs
and i can be honest with you
could it really be this simple
have i not been condemned
is this what it's like to build a foundation
i thought i only knew how to break them

i can't believe i settled
for scraps for so long
bits of affection
peppered with rejection
taught that the only way
i'd be worthy of love
was begging on my knees
with you it all comes so easily
i'm standing on my own two feet
i don't have to ask for anything

it's instinctual to me
to feel like love is finite
like if i love you with my whole heart
there's nothing left over
but i'm learning that
there's no limit on my capacity
i can love you with all of me
and still have so much more to give

you deserve a count on me love. a bring you coffee in the morning love. a makes you playlists kind of love. a play with your hair while you fall asleep kind of love. a stay in bed all day kind of love. a remembers your favourite things kind of love. a gift just cause it reminds them of you kind of love. a smiles at you for no reason kind of love. a brings you cookies when you have cramps kind of love. an understanding love. a love that wants to grow with you. a love that sees your unwashed hair, your crusty morning eyes, your overthinking, a love that loves you even more because of it. you deserve an unconditional love. a love that makes you feel safe.

i used to think i had to choose
one love language to prioritize
but effortlessly
you give me all five

YOU ARE SO EASY TO LOVE

thought i was better off alone
didn't need someone to rely on
thought another's presence
would never make things better
but then you walked in
smiled nervously
somehow saw me immediately
and now this one who thought
they might be forever lonely
has become part of a we

my nervous system is finally
learning what it's like to feel safe
check engine light off
maybe i was always ok
maybe there was never anything
wrong with me to begin with

in loving like this
i didn't know there would be
so much to grieve
for the past love i never received

falling in love
makes me feel like
i'm in my mother's body
when i look down
i see her hands
when i look in the mirror
i hear her voice in my head
feelings of unworthiness
are so loud
hyperindependence
screaming at me
how could she teach me
how to rely on someone
when she never could
how could she show me
what it feels like to be safe
when she never was

the inner child in me
sees the inner child in you

i got so used to stumbling
bending over backwards
falling
but when it's just
me and you
i finally feel like i'm landing

we had the darkest winter
in eighty years
but now the clouds are clearing
snow is melting
birds are chirping
there's daisies on my kitchen table
and a part of me thinks
i only made it through
because i had my sunshine
because i met you

i love how you look in the traffic lights
i'll drive you to work every night
your kiss goodbye
worth tired tomorrow
your *how did i get so lucky*
worth early mornings
the truth is for you
i'd drive thirty thousand miles
the truth is for you
there's nothing i wouldn't do

i'll show you what's hidden
even when it hurts
what's stored behind old boxes and shame
i'll open up to you
so you can embrace all my hard parts
if you promise to do the same

our love is late night kisses. eyes locked. movie dates. baking brownies. licking the spoon. our love is cut up strawberries. the first spring bloom. our love is a blanket that covers your shoulders. your hand on my knee. flowers just because. our love is sleepy sundays. my nose in your hair. our love is kinetic. our love has a pulse. our love is honey. lavender. silk. our love is warm. our love is soft. our love is endless. our love is ours.

i can't explain where
all my love for you
came from
it's as if we once
raised a child
baby fingers gripping pinkies
or died together on
a bed of daisies
it's as if i were the sun
and you were the moon
always convincing each other
the next day was worth rising for
and when i was too caught
up in being the ocean you
never forgot to remind me
what it feels like to burn
i can't believe we finally
collided in this century
cause i am certain i have
loved you in more than
a thousand different lifetimes

what an overwhelming
joy it is
to find your person
after not having one for so long

you make me so happy i don't have any words left

in my sweatpants era. in my chocolate chip pancakes for breakfast era. in my different nail designs on each hand era. in my middle part era. in my mochas with oat milk era. in my moving my body for no reason other than that it feels good era. in my things can work out better than i imagined even if it's not what i planned era. in my maybe i can grow into a greater version of me without worrying about doing it perfectly era. in my surrendering era. in my soft era. in my i know who is safe to let in era. in my self-trust era. in my letting myself be cared for era. in my realizing how much love exists in the universe era. in my lover era.

this is the first happy ending
i didn't have to force

i hope you create moments for yourself in every day. i hope you take deep breaths of fresh air. i hope you remind yourself you're alive. i hope you love. i hope you realize there are so many things in this life to be in love with. i hope you cherish yourself as much as your relationships. i hope you don't treat love like it's a secret. i hope you shout it from the rooftops. i hope you witness all the parts of yourself. i hope you hug your inner child as often as you can. i hope you remember that your purpose in life is to enjoy living. i hope you know that being yourself is enough. i hope you say no to the things that want to hold you back. i hope you feel free. and most of all, i hope you find peace.

about the author

michaela angemeer (she/they) is a queer canadian poet who's passionate about sharing her healing journey and inspiring readers to spend more time with their feelings.

they've published four best-selling collections of poetry including *when he leaves you, you'll come back to yourself, please love me at my worst* and *poems for the signs.*

michaela's newest book, *there is room for all of you here,* is an excavation of the past that leads to a celebration of queer love. separated into three sections: stumbling, falling, and landing, it's about complicated family relationships, reconciling with your insecure attachment style, finding a healthy love, and building something you hope will last.

michaela lives in kitchener, ontario with their frenchton, bea. you can find her at local coffee shops, her favourite wine bar, or in her backyard looking up at the moon.

get in touch on tiktok & instagram: @michaelapoetry
get the rest of their books: michaelapoetry.com